THIS BOOK BELONGS TO:

_____

_____

Shop our other books at
www.sillyslothpress.com

For questions and customer service, email us at
support@sillyslothpress.com

JOKE 1

Q: HOW CAN YOU TEACH YOUR KIDS ABOUT INCOME TAX?

A: EAT 30% OF THEIR ICE CREAM.

JOKE 2

Q: A RANCHER SENDS HIS ACCOUNTING SHEEPDOG, MAX, OFF TO GATHER HIS 7 SHEEP. ON RETURNING THE RANCHER IS SURPRISED TO SEE HE NOW HAS 10 SHEEP IN HIS PEN AND ASKS THE DOG TO EXPLAIN.

A: "WOOF! YOU ASKED ME TO ROUND THEM UP," BARKS MAX.

JOKE 3

Q: HOW DID THE AUDITOR PROPOSE TO HIS GIRLFRIEND?

A: WITH AN ENGAGEMENT LETTER.

JOKE 4

Q: WHAT DO YOU CALL A GROUP FINANCIAL CONTROLLER WHO'S LOST HIS JOB?

A: BOB.

JOKE 5

Q: WHAT IS THE PURPOSE OF AN FBAR?

A: TO SERVE IMPORTED BEER.

JOKE 6

Q: WHY DID THE AUDITOR CROSS THE ROAD?

A: BECAUSE HE LOOKED IN THE FILE AND THAT'S WHAT THEY DID LAST YEAR.

JOKE 7

Q: WHY DID THE DENTIST'S ACCOUNTANT GO TO PRISON?

A: FOR INCISOR TRADING.

JOKE 8

Q: DID YOU HEAR ABOUT THE CANNIBAL CPA?

A: SHE CHARGES AN ARM AND A LEG.

JOKE 9

Q: HOW DO YOU KNOW YOU HAVE AN UNETHICAL CPA?

A: YOU HEAR HIM ON THE PHONE SAYING, "SURE, MR. MADOFF, I AM GLAD TO DO THAT FOR YOU."

JOKE 10

Q: WHAT DO YOU CALL A FINANCIAL CONTROLLER WHO ALWAYS WORKS THROUGH LUNCH, TAKES TWO VACATION DAYS EVERY TWO YEARS, IS IN THE OFFICE EVERY SATURDAY, AND LEAVES EVERY NIGHT AFTER 10 P.M.?

A: A SLACKER.

JOKE 11

Q: WHERE DO SEAGULLS INVEST THEIR MONEY?

A: IN THE STORK MARKET!

JOKE 12

Q: WHAT IS AN ACCOUNTANT'S FAVORITE HOBBY?

A: TAXIDERMY.

JOKE 13

Q: WHY DO ACCOUNTANTS MAKE THE BEST LOVERS?

A: THEY'RE GREAT WITH FIGURES AND THEY'RE SKILLED AT DOUBLE ENTRY.

JOKE 14

Q: HOW CAN YOU TELL IF YOU HAVE A BAD FINANCIAL ADVISOR?

A: YOU TELL THEM TO BUY AOL STOCK AND THEY ASK YOU THE TICKER SYMBOL.

JOKE 15

Q: WHY DID THE BANKER LIKE THE TV SHOW?

A: BECAUSE HE WAS INVESTED IN THE STORY.

JOKE 16

Q: WHY DO ECONOMISTS EXIST?

A: SO ACCOUNTANTS HAVE SOMEONE TO MAKE JOKES ABOUT.

JOKE 17

Q: HOW DID THE BANKER DIE?

A: HE CASHED OUT.

JOKE 18

Q: WHY DON'T PEOPLE LIKE ACCOUNTANT JOKES?

A: THEY CAN HAVE ACCRUAL PUNCHLINE.

JOKE 19

Q: HOW CAN YOU RUIN AN ACCOUNTANT'S ENTIRE YEAR?

A: STRAP HIM TO A CHAIR, STAND IN FRONT OF HIM AND FOLD A ROAD MAP THE WRONG WAY.

JOKE 20

Q: WHY DID THE INVESTMENT BANKERS START DATING?

A: COMPOUND INTEREST.

Q: WHAT DO YOU CALL A BANKER WITHOUT FRIENDS?

A: A LOANER.

Q: WHAT IS AN ACTUARY?

A: AN ACCOUNTANT WITHOUT A SENSE OF HUMOR.

JOKE 23

Q: IF INTROVERTED ACCOUNTANTS STARE AT THEIR OWN SHOES, WHAT DO EXTROVERTED ACCOUNTANTS DO?

A: STARE AT YOUR SHOES.

JOKE 24

Q: WHAT DO YOU CALL AN ACCOUNTANT WITHOUT A SPREADSHEET?

A: LOST.

JOKE 25

Q: HOW DO YOU KNOW ACCOUNTANTS HAVE NO IMAGINATION?

A: THEY NAMED A FIRM PRICEWATERHOUSE-COOPERS.

JOKE 26

Q: WHAT WOULD YOU CALL ECONOMICS WITHOUT ASSUMPTIONS?

A: TAX ACCOUNTING.

JOKE 27

Q: WHY WAS THE AUDITOR HIT BY A CAR WHILE CROSSING THE STREET?

A: AUDITORS NEVER ACTUALLY DO THE RISK ASSESSMENT WELL UNTIL AFTER THE ACCIDENT HAPPENS.

JOKE 28

IT'S 4:04.

DO YOU KNOW WHERE YOUR AUDITOR IS?

JOKE 29

A GUY IN A BAR LEANS OVER TO THE GUY NEXT TO HIM AND SAYS, "WANT TO HEAR AN ACCOUNTANT JOKE?"

THE GUY NEXT TO HIM REPLIES, "WELL, BEFORE YOU TELL THAT JOKE, YOU SHOULD KNOW THAT I'M 6 FEET TALL, 200 POUNDS, AND I'M AN ACCOUNTANT. AND THE GUY SITTING NEXT TO ME IS 6 2" TALL, 225 POUNDS, AND HE'S AN ACCOUNTANT. NOW, DO YOU STILL WANT TO TELL THAT JOKE?"

THE FIRST GUY SAYS, "NO, I DON'T WANT TO HAVE TO EXPLAIN IT TWICE."

JOKE 30

Q: WHAT WOULD YOU EXPECT TO HEAR FROM A CONVERSATION BETWEEN TWO ACCOUNTANTS AT A COCKTAIL PARTY?

A: ".....AND NINTHLY....."

JOKE 31

Q: WHY CAN'T YOU FIND GOLD AT THE END OF A RAINBOW?

A: THE LEPRECHAUN SEIZED IT AND SOLD IT TO CASH4GOLD!

JOKE 32

Q: WHAT HAPPENS WHEN YOU TRAP AN ACCOUNTANT AND A HYENA IN A ROOM?

A: THE HYENA STOPS LAUGHING.

JOKE 33

"I HAVE BAD NEWS AND WORSE NEWS..." A FINANCIAL ADVISER SAYS TO HER CLIENT.

"WHICH WOULD YOU LIKE TO HEAR FIRST?"

"THE BAD NEWS," THE CLIENT SAYS.

"ALL YOUR MONEY WILL BE GONE IN 24 HOURS."

"OH MY GOSH," THE CLIENT SAYS. "WHAT'S THE WORSE NEWS?"

"I SHOULD HAVE MADE THIS CALL YESTERDAY."

JOKE 34

Q: WHEN DO ACCOUNTANTS LAUGH OUT LOUD?

A: WHEN SOMEBODY ASKS FOR A RAISE.

JOKE 35

Q: WHY ARE ACCOUNTANTS SO PATIENT, SOOTHING, AND SERENE?

A: BECAUSE THEY HAVE STRONG INTERNAL CONTROLS.

JOKE 36

Q: HOW WAS COPPER WIRE INVENTED?

A: TWO ACCOUNTANTS WERE ARGUING OVER A PENNY.

JOKE 37

Q: WHAT IS AN ACCOUNTANT?

A: SOMEONE WHO SOLVES A PROBLEM YOU DID NOT KNOW YOU HAD IN A WAY YOU DON'T UNDERSTAND.

JOKE 38

AN ACCOUNTANT WITH INSOMNIA SEES A DOCTOR.

ACCOUNTANT: "DOCTOR, I JUST CAN'T GET TO SLEEP AT NIGHT."

DOCTOR: "HAVE YOU TRIED COUNTING SHEEP?"

ACCOUNTANT: "THAT'S THE PROBLEM – I MAKE AN ERROR AND THEN SPEND 3 HOURS TRYING TO FIGURE IT OUT."

JOKE 39

Q: WHAT DOES CPA STAND FOR?

A: CAN'T PASS AGAIN.

JOKE 40

Q: WHY DID HE CROSS BACK?

A: SO HE COULD CHARGE THE CLIENT FOR TRAVEL EXPENSES.

JOKE 41

Q: HOW CAN YOU TELL IF YOUR KIDS ARE GOING TO BE TAX ACCOUNTANTS?

A: WHEN YOU READ THEM THE STORY OF CINDERELLA AND YOU GET TO THE PART WHERE THE PUMPKIN TURNS INTO A GOLDEN COACH, THEY ASK, "DADDY, IS THAT ORDINARY INCOME OR A LONG-TERM CAPITAL GAIN?"

JOKE 42

Q: DO YOU KNOW ABOUT THE DEVIANT FORENSIC ACCOUNTANT?

A: SHE GOT HER CLIENT'S CHARGES REDUCED FROM GROSS INDECENCY TO NET INDECENCY.

JOKE 43

Q: WHERE DO YOU REPORT UNDER THE TABLE INCOME?

A: BELOW THE LINE.

JOKE 44

Q: DID YOU HEAR ABOUT THE BLONDE MANAGEMENT ACCOUNTANT?

A: SHE WENT TO SEE HER PERSONAL TRAINER TO DISCUSS STRETCH TARGETS.

JOKE 45

Q: WHAT'S THE DIFFERENCE BETWEEN AN ECONOMIST AND A CONFUSED OLD MAN WITH ALZHEIMER'S?

A: THE ECONOMIST IS THE ONE WITH A CALCULATOR.

JOKE 46

Q: HOW DID THE ACCOUNTANT REACT WHEN SHE RECEIVED A BLANK CHECK?

A: "MY DEDUCTIONS HAVE AT LAST CAUGHT UP WITH THE SALARY."

JOKE 47

Q: WHAT KIND OF HUMOR DO ACCOUNTANTS ENJOY?

A: SELF-DEPRECIATING.

JOKE 48

Q: WHAT DID THE ACCOUNTANT TELL HER FRIEND WHO LOST HER JOB AS A PSYCHIC?

A: YOU DIDN'T SEE THAT ONE COMING DID YOU.

JOKE 49

Q: ASK A LAWYER WHAT 2+2 IS AND HE'LL SAY 5, ASK AN ENGINEER AND HE'LL SAY 4, ASK AN ACCOUNTANT AND WHAT WILL HE SAY?

A: "WHAT DO YOU WANT IT TO BE?"

JOKE 50

Q: WHAT DOES IT MEAN WHEN AN ACCOUNTANT IS DROOLING FROM BOTH SIDES OF HER MOUTH?

A: HER DESK IS LEVEL.

JOKE 51

Q: WHY DOES SANTA LIKE TRAVELING TO THE UK?

A: HE CAN CLAIM GIFT RELIEF.

JOKE 52

Q: WHY ARE ACCOUNTING DEPARTMENTS SO FRIENDLY?

A: BECAUSE EVERYONE COUNTS.

JOKE 53

Q: HOW MANY ACCOUNTANTS DOES IT TAKE TO CHANGE A LIGHT BULB?

A: HOW MUCH MONEY DO YOU HAVE?

JOKE 54

Q: WHAT IS A TAX TABLE?

A: A PLACE TO NEGOTIATE WITH THE IRS.

Q: HOW DO ACCOUNTANTS TRASH A HOTEL ROOM?

A: THEY REFUSE TO FILL OUT THE GUEST COMMENT CARD.

Q: WHAT'S THE DIFFERENCE BETWEEN A $25 STEAK AND A $60 STEAK?

A: FEBRUARY 14TH.

JOKE 57

Q: WHAT IS THE ACCOUNTANT'S PRAYER?

A: LORD, HELP ME BE MORE RELAXED ABOUT TRIVIAL DETAILS, STARTING TOMORROW AT 11.24:07 AM, EASTERN DAYLIGHT-SAVING TIME.

JOKE 58

Q: WHY DID THE ENRON EMPLOYEE CLAIM SHE SAW A GHOST ON HALLOWEEN?

A: A CHILD DRESSED UP AS A 401 (K)

JOKE 59

Q: HOW DO YOU KNOW WHEN THE CHIEF ACCOUNTANT IS GETTING SOFT?

A: WHEN HE ACTUALLY LISTENS TO MARKETING BEFORE SAYING "NO".

JOKE 60

Q: WHAT IS A BANK?

A: A PLACE THAT WILL LEND YOU MONEY ONLY IF YOU CAN PROVE THAT YOU DON'T NEED IT.

JOKE 61

ACCOUNTING FOR DUMMIES. WHAT'S THE BIG DEAL? CR. CASH DR. DUMMIES. SIMPLE.

JOKE 62

Q: WHAT'S A SHY AND RETIRING TAX ACCOUNTANT?

A: A TAX ACCOUNTANT WHO IS HALF A MILLION SHY AND THAT'S WHY HE'S RETIRING.

JOKE 63

Q: WHAT DID THE ACCOUNTANT TELL THE ACROBAT?

A: "YOU HAVE SOME OUTSTANDING BALANCE!"

JOKE 64

Q: IF YOU WANT TO GET RICH, WHY SHOULD YOU KEEP QUIET?

A: BECAUSE SILENCE IS GOLDEN.

JOKE 65

Q: WHAT IS THE DEFINITION OF AN ECONOMIST?

A: SOMEONE WHO DIDN'T HAVE ENOUGH PERSONALITY TO BECOME AN ACCOUNTANT.

JOKE 66

Q: HOW CAN YOU TELL IF A TENNIS PLAYER IS SUCCESSFUL?

A: THEY HAVE A LOT OF NET INCOME.

JOKE 67

Q: WHY IS AMERICA THE LAND OF OPPORTUNITY?

A: EVERYONE CAN BE A TAXPAYER.

JOKE 68

Q: WHAT DO YOU CALL A PERSON WITH A HEAD FULL OF COINS?

A: HEADQUARTERS.

JOKE 69

Q: DID YOU HEAR OF THE ECONOMIST WHO DOVE INTO HIS SWIMMING POOL AND BROKE HIS NECK?

A: HE FORGOT TO SEASONALLY ADJUST.

JOKE 70

Q: WHAT KIND OF CANDY DO BANKERS LIKE?

A: INVESTMINTS.

JOKE 71

Q: WHAT CONDITION DO ACCOUNTANTS SUFFER FROM?

A: DEPRECIATION.

JOKE 72

Q: WHAT DO ACCOUNTANTS LOVE THE MOST ABOUT HOLIDAYS?

A: LESS TRAFFIC DURING THEIR COMMUTE.

JOKE 73

Q: WHY WAS ASTROLOGY INVENTED?

A: SO ECONOMICS WOULD SEEM LIKE AN ACCURATE SCIENCE.

JOKE 74

Q: IF AN ACCOUNTANT'S WIFE CAN'T GET TO SLEEP, WHAT DOES SHE DO?

A: LEANS OVER TO HER HUSBAND AND SAYS, "TELL ME ABOUT WORK TODAY, HONEY."

JOKE 75

Q: WHAT SUPERPOWER WOULD AN ACCOUNTANT WISH FOR?

A: TELEPATHY WITH AN EXCEL SPREADSHEET.

JOKE 76

Q: HOW DO PIRATES REPORT THEIR TAXES?

A: ON THE SCHEDULE SEA.

Q: HOW CAN YOU TELL WHEN IT'S COLD OUTSIDE?

A: IF YOU SEE A STOCKBROKER WALKING WITH HIS HANDS IN HIS OWN POCKETS.

Q: DID YOU KNOW ECONOMISTS HAVE PREDICTED NINE OUT OF THE LAST FIVE RECESSIONS?

JOKE 79

Q: HOW CAN YOU TELL YOU'VE FOUND A GOOD TAX ACCOUNTANT?

A: HE HAS A LOOPHOLE NAMED AFTER HIM.

JOKE 80

Q: HOW DO THUNDERSTORMS INVEST THEIR MONEY?

A: IN A COMBINATION OF LIQUID AND FROZEN ASSETS.

JOKE 81

Q: HOW DID BERNIE MADOFF GET THE IDEA FOR A PONZI SCHEME?

A: SOCIAL SECURITY.

JOKE 82

Q: WHY DID THE ACCOUNTANT FALL OFF A CLIFF?

A: SHE LOST HER BALANCE.

JOKE 83

Q: WHERE DO ACCOUNTANTS SHOP FOR CLOTHES?

A: GAAP

JOKE 84

Q: WHY WAS THE CANNIBAL FINANCIAL ADVISER REPRIMANDED?

A: FOR BUTTERING UP HER CLIENTS.

JOKE 85

A CLIENT ASKS HIS ADVISER, "IS ALL MY MONEY REALLY GONE?"

"NO, OF COURSE NOT," THE ADVISER SAYS.

"IT'S JUST WITH SOMEBODY ELSE!"

JOKE 86

Q: WHAT DOES AIG SIGNIFY?

A: AND IT'S GONE!

Q: WHAT ARE THE TWO RULES FOR CREATING A SUCCESSFUL ACCOUNTING BUSINESS?

A: 1. DON'T TELL THEM EVERYTHING YOU KNOW.
2. [REDACTED]

Q: HOW CAN YOU PREVENT A BULL FROM CHARGING?

A: CANCEL HIS CREDIT CARD.

JOKE 89

Q: HOW HAS FRENCH REVOLUTION INFLUENCED WORLD ECONOMIC GROWTH?

A: TOO EARLY TO SAY.

JOKE 90

Q: WHY SHOULDN'T YOU PICK A FIGHT WITH AN ACCOUNTANT?

A: THEY'LL ALWAYS OUTNUMBER YOU.

JOKE 91

Q: WHAT IS A FAILSAFE FORM OF BIRTH CONTROL FOR AN ACCOUNTANT?

A: THEIR PERSONALITY.

JOKE 92

Q: HOW CAN YOU DESTROY AN ACCOUNTANT'S SANITY?

A: TIE THEM TO A CHAIR AND MESS UP THEIR EXCEL FORMULAS.

JOKE 93

Q: WHY ARE HIPPIES GOOD ACCOUNTANTS?

A: BECAUSE THEY'RE FROM COUNTERCULTURE.

JOKE 94

Q: WHY SHOULD YOU BORROW MONEY FROM PESSIMISTS?

A: THEY DON'T EXPECT YOU TO REPAY.

JOKE 95

Q: HOW MANY ADVISERS DOES IT TAKE TO SCREW IN A LIGHTBULB?

A: ONE TO HIRE A LIGHTBULB INSTALLER TO DO IT AND THEN CHARGE YOU 1% OF YOUR ASSETS EACH YEAR.

JOKE 96

Q: DID YOU HEAR ABOUT THE FRAUDULENT IRISH FINANCE DIRECTOR?

A: HE BURNED HIS OFFICE DOWN TRYING TO COOK THE BOOKS.

JOKE 97

Q: HOW DO ACCOUNTANTS DRESS AT COCKTAIL PARTIES?

A: WEAR THEIR DARK GREY SOCKS INSTEAD OF THE LIGHT GREY.

JOKE 98

Q: HOW DOES SANTA'S ACCOUNTANT VALUE HIS SLEIGH?

A: NET PRESENT VALUE.

JOKE 99

Q: WHAT DID THE SCHIZOPHRENIC ACCOUNTANT SAY?

A: I HEAR INVOICES!

JOKE 100

Q: WHAT DO ACCOUNTANTS ALWAYS ASK ON THE FIRST DATE?

A: "DO YOU HAVE AN ALLOWANCE FOR DOUBTFUL DECISIONS?"

JOKE 101

Q: WHY DID THE ACCOUNTANT WET HIS PANTS?

A: HE LACKED INTERNAL CONTROLS.

JOKE 102

Q: WHAT IS THE DEFINITION OF UNLIKELY?

A: A PHOTOSPREAD IN PLAYBOY TITLED THE WORLD'S TOP ACCOUNTANTS — NUDE!

JOKE 103

Q: WHAT ARE THE THREE TYPES OF ACCOUNTANTS?

A: THOSE WHO CAN COUNT AND THOSE WHO CANNOT.

JOKE 104

Q: WHAT SPORT DO ACCOUNTANTS LIKE TO PLAY DURING THE BUSY SEASON?

A: ULTIMATE FASB.

JOKE 105

Q: WHAT IS THE DIFFERENCE BETWEEN TAX AVOIDANCE AND TAX EVASION?

A: JAIL.

JOKE 106

Q: WHY DON'T ACCOUNTANTS ENJOY NOVELS?

A: BECAUSE THE ONLY NUMBERS IN THEM ARE PAGE NUMBERS.

JOKE 107

Q: IF THE PESSIMIST SEES THE GLASS HALF EMPTY AND THE OPTIMIST SEES IT HALF FULL, WHAT DOES THE FINANCIAL ADVISOR SEE?

A: THE PERFECT TIME TO ADD WHISKEY.

JOKE 108

Q: WHAT IS QDOT.COM?

A: A FOREIGN MATCHMAKING SERVICE.

JOKE 109

Q: WHAT DO YOU CALL IT WHEN YOU LET A BISON BORROW MONEY?

A: BUFF-A-LOAN!

JOKE 110

Q: WHAT IS AN ACCOUNTANT'S BEST PICKUP LINE?

A: YOU REALLY KNOW HOW TO WORK YOUR §751(C)S AND (D)S.

JOKE 111

Q: WHAT DO YOU CALL AN ACCOUNTANT WHO LOST THEIR CALCULATOR?

A: LONELY.

JOKE 112

Q: WHAT IS AN ACCOUNTANT'S BEST DEFENSE?

A: "WE'RE NOT BORING PEOPLE, WE JUST GET EXCITED OVER BORING THINGS."

JOKE 113

Q: WHY IS DOUGH A SYNONYM FOR MONEY?

A: BECAUSE EVERYONE KNEADS IT.

JOKE 114

SENIOR: LOOK AT LAST YEAR AND DO THAT.

SENIOR WHEN REVIEWING: WHY DIDN'T YOU INCLUDE THIS ACCOUNT?

STAFF: BECAUSE THEY DIDN'T INCLUDE IT LAST YEAR.

SENIOR: JUST BECAUSE THEY DID IT THAT WAY LAST YEAR DOESN'T MEAN IT WAS RIGHT.

STAFF: ......

JOKE 115

Q: HOW DO RURAL BANKERS SPEAK?

A: WITHDRAWL

JOKE 116

Q: HOW CAN YOU TELL WHEN AN ACCOUNTANT IS ON VACATION?

A: HE DOESN'T WEAR A TIE AND COMES IN AFTER 8AM.

JOKE 117

Q: WHAT DO YOU CALL AN ACCOUNTANT WHO CLAIMS THEY POSTED A ONE-SIDED JOURNAL?

A: A LIAR! UNDER SARBOX RULES IT JUST CAN'T HAPPEN! CAN IT?!?

JOKE 118

Q: WHY WAS THE ACCOUNTANT SO THRILLED WHEN SHE FINISHED A PUZZLE IN ONLY 58 WEEKS?

A: BECAUSE ON THE BOX IT SAID 6-12 YEARS.

JOKE 119

Q: WHY AREN'T ACCOUNTANTS EVER INVITED TO COMPANY SWIM PARTIES?

A: THEIR JOB REQUIRES THAT THEY POINT OUT ANY SHRINKAGE.

JOKE 120

Q: WHAT'S GREY, HAS 6 LEGS, 2 ARMS, AND IS TWENTY FEET TALL?

A: AN ACCOUNTANT RIDING AN ELEPHANT.

JOKE 121

Q: WHY DID THE ACCOUNTANT GO TO REHAB?

A: SOLVENCY ABUSE.

JOKE 122

Q: WHAT DO YOU CALL AN INVESTMENT THAT PROFITS OFF SHAREHOLDER ACTIVISM?

A: THE "FEELING IS MUTUAL FUND".

JOKE 123

Q: WHEN DOES A PERSON DECIDE TO BECOME A STOCKBROKER?

A: WHEN SHE REALIZES SHE DOESN'T HAVE THE CHARISMA TO SUCCEED AS AN UNDERTAKER.

JOKE 124

Q: HOW DOES AN ACCOUNTANT STAY OUT OF DEBT?

A: HE LEARNS TO ACT HIS WAGE.

JOKE 125

Q: WHAT DOES AN ACCOUNTANT SAY WHEN BOARDING THE SUBWAY?

A: "MIND THE GAAP."

JOKE 126

Q: WHAT IS AN AUDITOR?

A: SOMEONE WHO ARRIVES AFTER THE BATTLE AND BAYONETS THE WOUNDED.

JOKE 127

Q: HOW DO PET STORES REPORT INVENTORY?

A: USING THE FIFO METHOD.

JOKE 128

Q: WHAT'S THE DIFFERENCE BETWEEN DEATH AND TAXES?

A: CONGRESS DOESN'T MEET ANNUALLY TO MAKE DEATH WORSE.

JOKE 129

Q: WHY DID THE ACCOUNTANT DIVORCE THE BANKER?

A: THEY COULDN'T RECONCILE THEIR DIFFERENCES.

JOKE 130

FOUR LAWS OF ACCOUNTING:

1. TRIAL BALANCES DON'T.

2. BANK RECONCILIATIONS NEVER DO.

3. WORKING CAPITAL DOES NOT.

4. RETURN ON INVESTMENTS NEVER WILL.

JOKE 131

Q: WHY DID THE ACCOUNTANT START SMOKING?

A: SO HE CAN DEDUCT CIGARETTES FROM HIS INCOME TAX AND CALL IT A LOSS BY FIRE. THUS, HIS MEDICAL EXPENSES WENT ABOVE THE 71/2% THRESHOLD.

JOKE 132

Q: WHY WAS JANET JACKSON'S ACCOUNTANT SO DISAPPOINTED WHEN SHE HAD A WARDROBE MALFUNCTION?

A: BECAUSE TO HIM, IT WAS A MATERIAL WEAKNESS.

JOKE 133

Q: WHAT IS A BUDGET?

A: AN ORDERLY SYSTEM FOR LIVING BEYOND YOUR MEANS.

JOKE 134

Q: WHERE DO FISH STORE THEIR MONEY?

A: IN THE RIVERBANK.

JOKE 135

Q: WHO WAS THE FIRST TAX ACCOUNTANT?

A: ADAM. HE GOT INTERESTED IN FIGURES, TURNED THE FIRST LEAF, MADE THE FIRST ENTRY, LOST INTEREST AFTER WITHDRAWAL, BUGGERED UP THE MONTHLY ACCOUNTS AND RAISED THE FIRST TAX LIABILITY.

JOKE 136

Q: WHY DID THE BANKER QUIT HER JOB?

A: SHE LOST INTEREST.

JOKE 137

SOME SAY THAT NOBODY SHOULD KEEP TOO MUCH TO THEMSELVES.

THE IRS OFFICE IS OF THE SAME OPINION.

JOKE 138

Q: HOW MANY ECONOMISTS DOES IT TAKE TO CHANGE A LIGHT BULB?

A: SEVEN, PLUS/MINUS TEN.

JOKE 139

Q: WHAT DID THE CPA SAY WHEN HE SAW THE TAX FORM?

A: THE MAN WHO SET THE STANDARD DEDUCTION MUST HAVE BEEN A BACHELOR. IT'S A LIE WHEN I LIST MYSELF AS THE HEAD OF HOUSEHOLD.

JOKE 140

Q: WHAT HAPPENED TO THE CONSTIPATED ACCOUNTANT?

A: HE COULDN'T BUDGET, SO HE HAD TO WORK IT OUT WITH A PENCIL.

JOKE 141

Q: WHY WOULD THANOS MAKE A GREAT ACCOUNTANT?

A: BECAUSE THE BOOKS WOULD ALWAYS BE BALANCED.

JOKE 142

Q: HOW DO ACCOUNTANTS UNWIND?

A: ADD THE TELEPHONE BOOK.

JOKE 143

Q: WHY DO SOME ACCOUNTANTS DECIDE TO BECOME ACTUARIES?

A: THEY FIND BOOKKEEPING TOO EXCITING.

JOKE 144

Q: WHAT IS AN ACCOUNTANT'S FAVORITE PLACE TO TAKE COVER?

A: IN A TAX SHELTER.

JOKE 145

Q: WHAT ARE FAST FOOD EMPLOYEES NOW ASKING CUSTOMERS?

A: CAN YOU AFFORD FRIES WITH THAT?

JOKE 146

Q: WHAT'S GREY AND NOT THERE?

A: AN ACCOUNTANT ON HOLIDAY.

JOKE 147

Q: WHAT COIN DOUBLES IN VALUE WHEN HALF IS DEDUCTED?

A: A HALF DOLLAR.

JOKE 148

Q: WHAT DO ACCOUNTANTS SAY WHEN YOU ASK THEM THE TIME?

A: IT'S 8:34AM AND 17 SECONDS; NO WAIT 18 SECONDS, NO WAIT 19 SECONDS, NO WAIT...

JOKE 149

Q: WHAT'S GREY ON THE INSIDE AND RED ON THE OUTSIDE?

A: AN ACCOUNTANT FLIPPED INSIDE OUT.

JOKE 150

Q: WHERE CAN YOU BUY CHICKEN BROTH IN BULK?

A: THE STOCK MARKET.

JOKE 151

Q: WHY DID THE ACCOUNTANT BUY NEW BALANCES?

A: SO HE COULD TIE HIS SHOES.

JOKE 152

Q: WHY DID THE MAN BURY HIS MONEY IN SNOW?

A: HE WANTED COLD HARD CASH.

JOKE 153

Q: HOW DO YOU MAKE A MILLION DOLLARS TRADING PENNY STOCKS?

A: START WITH 2 MILLION.

JOKE 154

Q: WHAT DO YOU CALL A TRIAL BALANCE THAT DOESN'T BALANCE?

A: A LATE NIGHT.

JOKE 155

Q: WHY DID THE ACCOUNTANT PRINT OUT 50 SHEETS OF CLEAN, SPOTLESS PAPER?

A: SHE SAID SHE NEEDED 50 BLANK SHEETS AND DID NOT WANT TO COUNT THEM MANUALLY.

JOKE 156

Q: WHAT DO YOU GET WHEN YOU PUT THE MONEY YOU'VE WORKED FOR AND IRS TOGETHER?

A: THEIRS!

JOKE 157

Q: WHY ARE NUDISTS BAD FOR THE STOCK MARKET?

A: BECAUSE THEY'RE ASSOCIATED WITH BARE MARKETS.

JOKE 158

Q: WHAT IS THE ARMY SLOGAN FOR ACCOUNTANTS?

A: BE AUDIT YOU CAN BE.

JOKE 159

Q: WHAT'S ANOTHER NAME FOR LONG-TERM INVESTMENT?

A: A FAILED SHORT-TERM INVESTMENT.

JOKE 160

Q: WHAT DO YOU CALL A COMPANY THAT IS RUN BY A KID?

A: BABY ON BOARD OF DIRECTORS.

JOKE 161

Q: WHY DO WE CALL FINANCIAL ADVISER'S EXPERTS?

A: HE WILL KNOW TOMORROW WHY THE THINGS HE PREDICTED YESTERDAY DIDN'T HAPPEN TODAY.

JOKE 162

Q: DID YOU HEAR THE IRS NOW OFFERS A TAX CREDIT ON THE PURCHASE OF CANNABIS?

A: YOU JUST NEED TO FILE A JOINT RETURN.

JOKE 163

A WOMAN WENT TO THE DOCTOR WHO TOLD HER SHE ONLY HAD 6 MONTHS TO LIVE.

"OH NO!" SAID THE WOMAN. "WHAT SHALL I DO?"

"MARRY AN ACCOUNTANT," SUGGESTED THE DOCTOR.

"WHY?" ASKED THE WOMAN. "WILL THAT MAKE ME LIVE LONGER?"

"NO," REPLIED THE DOCTOR. "BUT IT WILL SEEM LONGER."

JOKE 164

Q: WHAT HAPPENED TO THE ACCOUNTANT WHO ATE BAD THAI FOOD?

A: HE HAD TO LIQUIDATE HIS ASSETS.

JOKE 165

Q: WHAT'S THE ISSUE WITH BANKER JOKES?

A: BANKERS DON'T FIND THEM FUNNY AND NORMAL PEOPLE DON'T THINK THEY'RE JOKES.

JOKE 166

Q: HOW MANY CONSERVATIVE ECONOMISTS DOES IT TAKE TO SCREW IN A LIGHT BULB?

A: NONE. EVENTUALLY, THE DARKNESS WILL MAKE THE LIGHT BULB SCREW ITSELF IN.

JOKE 167

Q: WHY DO BANKERS GET THE BLUES?

A: THEY ALWAYS DRINK A LOAN.

JOKE 168

Q: WHY IS IT SO CHALLENGING FOR RESTAURANTS TO FIND CPAS?

A: BECAUSE THERE'S NO ACCOUNTING FOR TASTE.

JOKE 169

Q: WHAT DO YOU GET WHEN YOU CROSS A BANKER WITH A FISH?

A: A LOAN SHARK.

JOKE 170

Q: WHAT MUSIC IS PLAYED AT A FINANCIAL ACCOUNTANT'S FUNERAL?

A: THE LAST POST.

JOKE 171

Q: IF A FINE IS A TAX FOR DOING WRONG, WHAT IS A TAX?

A: A TAX IS A FINE FOR DOING WELL.

JOKE 172

Q: IF ACCOUNTANTS DON'T DIE, WHAT HAPPENS TO THEM?

A: THEY GET DERECOGNIZED.

Q: WHAT DO YOU CALL AN ACCOUNTANT WHO IS SEEN TALKING TO SOMEONE?

A: POPULAR.

Q: WHAT DID THE DUCK SAY WHEN HE ORDERED A ROUND OF DRINKS?

A: PUT IT ON MY BILL!

JOKE 175

Q: WHY DID THEY NAME IT A FORM 1040?

A: FOR EVERY $50 YOU EARN, YOU GET $10, THEY GET $40.

JOKE 176

Q: WHAT DID THE OVERWORKED ASSET SAY TO THE OTHER ASSET?

A: I FEEL SO UNDER DEPRECIATED.

JOKE 177

Q: WHY DOES PRE-TAX INCOME DISGUST ACCOUNTANTS?

A: IT'S GROSS.

JOKE 178

Q: WHY ARE SKUNKS EXEMPT FROM TAXES?

A: BECAUSE THEY ONLY HAVE ONE SCENT.

JOKE 179

Q: WHAT BOOK DO ACCOUNTANTS LIKE TO READ?

A: 50 SHADES OF GREY.

JOKE 180

Q: WHAT IS AN ILIT?

A: A TRUST CREATED BY A DRUNK.

JOKE 181

A STOCKBROKER WAS COMPLETING A JOB APPLICATION WHEN HE CAME TO THE QUESTION: "HAVE YOU EVER BEEN ARRESTED?" HE ANSWERED NO TO THE QUESTION. THE FOLLOWING QUESTION, INTENDED FOR THOSE WHO ANSWERED THE PRECEDING QUESTION WITH A YES, WAS "WHY?" NEVERTHELESS, THE STOCKBROKER ANSWERED IT "NEVER GOT CAUGHT."

Q: WHAT'S THE BEST WAY TO CLOSE GUANTANAMO BAY?

A: TURN IT INTO A BANK.

Q: HOW CAN YOU TELL WHEN AN ACCOUNTANT IS HAVING AN EXISTENTIAL CRISIS?

A: THEY GET A FASTER CALCULATOR.

JOKE 184

Q: WHY DID THE THIEF ONLY STEAL 1% OF THE BANK'S MONEY?

A: SHE WAS A FINANCIAL ADVISOR.

JOKE 185

Q: WHAT DOES FCPA STAND FOR?

A: FINALLY CAUGHT PINCHING THE ASSETS.

JOKE 186

A CLIENT HIRES A PRIVATE INVESTIGATOR TO FIND A MISSING ACCOUNTANT. THE INVESTIGATOR TELLS HIM THAT HE NEEDS A DESCRIPTION AND ASKS A FEW QUESTIONS. "WAS HE TALL OR WAS HE SHORT?"

THE CLIENT REPLIES, "BOTH!"

JOKE 187

Q: WHY DID WELLS FARGO WANT TO RETURN ALL THE GOVERNMENT BAILOUT MONEY ASAP?

A: THEY WERE UPSET AT ALL THE HIDDEN FEES.

Q: HOW DID THE FINANCIAL ADVISOR SLEEP LIKE A BABY DURING THE MARKET CRASH?

A: SHE WOKE UP EVERY HOUR AND CRIED.

Q: HOW DOES A TAX ACCOUNTANT SAY THE F-WORD?

A: "TRUST ME"

JOKE 190

Q: "WHEN THERE'S A WILL, THERE'S A _____?"

A: TAX SHELTER.

JOKE 191

Q: WHEN DOES IT RAIN MONEY?

A: WHEN THERE IS "CHANGE" IN THE WEATHER.

JOKE 192

Q: WHAT KIND OF CURRENCY DO CRABS USE?

A: SAND DOLLARS.

JOKE 193

Q: HOW MANY BANKERS DOES IT TAKE TO CHANGE A LIGHT BULB?

A: TWO. ONE TO REMOVE THE BULB AND DROP IT, AND THE OTHER TO TRY AND SELL IT BEFORE IT CRASHES (KNOWING THAT IT'S ALREADY BURNED OUT).

JOKE 194

Q: WHY ARE IRISH BANKERS SO SUCCESSFUL?

A: BECAUSE THEIR CAPITAL'S ALWAYS DUBLIN.

Q: HOW CAN A CPA TELL IF THEIR CLIENT IS AN ENGINEER?

A: IF EVERY NUMBER ON THEIR TAX RETURN IS WRONG BECAUSE THE VALUES HAD BEEN ROUNDED.

Q: HOW CAN YOU MAKE PEOPLE CARE ABOUT YOU?

A: MISS A COUPLE OF CREDIT CARD PAYMENTS.

JOKE 197

Q: WHY DID THE ACCOUNTANT EAT HIS CALCULATOR?

A: HE WAS A NUMBER CRUNCHER.

JOKE 198

Q: HOW DOES A PIRATE REPORT ALL THE TREASURE HE STOLE?

A: THEY HAVE A 1099-ARRRRRR FOR THAT.

JOKE 199

Q: HOW HAS THE ECONOMIC DOWNTURN INFLUENCED EATING HABITS?

A: THE 5-SECOND RULE IS NOW THE 5-MINUTE RULE!

JOKE 200

Q: WHAT DO STOCKBROKERS SAY TO EACH OTHER WHEN THEY WANT SILENCE?

A: PUT A STOCK IN IT.

JOKE 201

A CLIENT ASKS HER FINANCIAL ADVISER, "WHERE SHOULD I INVEST MY MONEY?"

"INVEST IN BOOZE," THE ADVISER SAYS. "WHERE ELSE DO YOU GET 40%?"

JOKE 202

Q: WHY DID THE ACCOUNTANT STARE AT A CUP OF ORANGE JUICE FOR THREE HOURS?

A: BECAUSE ON THE BOX IT SAID CONCENTRATE.

JOKE 203

Q: WHAT IS ODD ABOUT THE MARKET?

A: EVERY TIME ONE GUY SELLS, ANOTHER ONE BUYS, AND THEY BOTH THINK THEY'RE SMART.

JOKE 204

Q: HOW DO CPA'S LIKE TO BREAK THE ICE?

A: WOW, YOU HAVE A LOVELY SET OF W2S.

Q: WHY DO BANKERS MAKE GREAT LOVERS?

A: THEY KNOW THE PENALTY FOR EARLY WITHDRAWALS.